WHEN THE TWO MET

TO LOVE, LOSE AND LOVE AGAIN!

SUDARSHANA B. MUDALEYAR

This book is dedicated specifically to those who believe that love once lost is never found again.

Contents

Foreword

Having lost the love of my life, I relate much to this book: the aftermath, the heartbreak, the sorrow.

I lost what it felt like to be loved when I lost him, but love does find a way.

Sometimes, with the same person, and sometimes, with another.

When I first read this book, I was going through a heartbreak, and it left me gruesomely in emotional pain - I am sure anyone losing a loved one would know the feeling especially when one has planned a future with their significant other, but it all fades away.

Whilst reading this story, I realized that once loved does not mean all lost, maybe it might feel at the moment, but as time passes, we learn to live again, and find someone even better! Even if it could be the same person, it is just a better version of who they were in the past.

I'd recommend reading this one, it is just wholesome.

-Emona S. de Souza

Preface

Being in love as an experience differs from one person to another.

What I've written is purely fictional, but the emotions behind what is written stays true.

Love can be difficult, but it's an exhilarating experience too.

I've tried to capture the essence of the feeling in this story, and hope it catches the attention of the reader in a way that they can relate to it,

I'm more than happy to finally have written this book and publish it.

I never saw this day coming because writing was just my comfort zone through which I could just express and keep it to myself only.

Now, here I am, having written a full fledged anthology, purely based on my imagination, which I now present to you all.

Hope y'all love it :)

Acknowledgements

I would like to thank my parents, first and foremost, for all the support they have given.

To all my friends, who helped me through this journey and inspired me to write this one - thank you all!

And last, but not least, I would like to thank Emona S. de Souza for her inputs, edits and the proofreading.

Prologue

Chapter 1

TO LOVE

In that bustling city,

Lived two people,

Unknown to each other.

Both thinking of how it would be:

To find their soulmate,

And fall in love with them.

Feeling lonely and empty on the inside,

But pretending to be happy on the outside -

A feeling one would never wish to experience.

Wanting someone to talk to,

Wanting someone to listen to,

Wanting someone to cuddle with;

Not fearing the world around them,

They made up their minds,

Desperately waiting to meet the other.

But they didn't know

What they were about to face,

After they would meet.

A wild impending storm

Would hit their life.

One which was completely unknown to them:
Mixed emotions would rush through their veins.
But their encounter was still to be
A long-awaited one.
From sharing the same interests,
To wanting to achieve the same things in life,
All of it, would go hand in hand.
Their relationship could be likened
To a match made in heaven:
Soulmates made for one another.
Finally, the day had come:
Romance filled the air,
As if it was all pre-planned.
The calming sunlight hit their faces,
Making them look adorable.
Soft breeze ran through their hair.
And that was the moment
When they glanced at the other,
For the very first time!
Looking into each other's brown eyes,
They were lost in them -
And that was it.
They felt a spark,
One which was phenomenal,
Like they had never experienced before.
A brief moment was all it took:
Their eyes gazed deep into the other,

With a sweet yet soft smile.

They had never met earlier,

Yet upon introducing themselves,

They felt something deep inside.

As they continued talking,

They felt butterflies in their stomach:

And before they knew it - there it was!

A strange incomprehensible feeling:

But at the same time,

A magical one.

They couldn't shift their gazes from the other -

Even for a second!

And thus, it all began from there.

They immediately fell in love:

Overwhelmed by each other's aura,

As if it was all pre-determined.

Their feelings and emotions were all set:

But little did they know,

They had a long way to go.

Planning their next meeting

Seemed to be verv exciting,

And they were both looking forward to it.

After their first meet-up,

Evervthing seemed to be beautiful:

Love was in the air.

Their first meeting,

Was indeed dazzling!

And they wanted more of it.
The day of their first official date finally was here:
Both were eager and looking forward to it,
Both wanting to look their best.
She chose her most prepossessing outfit: a cute black dress,
Her hair was left open, as it caressed her face;
She layered it with an expensive musky French fragrance.
He was rather undecisive on what to wear because of the excitement.
Finally, he decided to go with a classic white shirt,
Pairing it with black chinos, he topped it off with a deep scent.
It was a small yet pretty café:
When the two were offered their seats,
It felt like a dream coming true.
Reality hit differently,
When the waiter asked them for their order,
And she shyly giggled.
Soon that café became home to
Long conversations, never-ending talks and debates:
They just loved being in each other's company.
Through those endless online chats and calls,
To their countless dates,
They fell deeply in love.
They wanted to be by each other's side
From sharing the good days,
To being there for the other during bad times.
Their unsaid promise was made:

With a subtle kiss
On the lips.
The promise was meant to be kept,
And it was certain to them,
That it will surely be kept.
Good things always come
In an unimaginable way,
And they do hit you differently;
Everything happens beyond your imagination
When you least expect it to happen.
As easy as it can come, it can also fade.
Nevertheless, everything that is unbelievable,
Doesn't stay for long.
Barriers always strike midway.
Maybe it's a sign,
Maybe it's your destiny,
Maybe it's a gut feeling.
Somewhere down the line,
If it's meant to happen, it will.
That is exactly how life works!
The first date is always exceptional -
Always a memorable one.
Neither can forget it for the rest of their lives.
Tucking her hair behind her ear.
Pointing out at that "coffee moustache".
Smiling at his dimple.
Such moments are so dreamy,

And carrying all of this forward

Is not everyone's cup of tea.

Everything went on smoothly.

Everything was felt in a jocular mood.

Everything seemed just perfect.

Such simple small coffee dates made them content.

Until one day, a seemingly sad incident hit their lives,

Which completely turned their lives upside down.

Chapter 02: To Lose

It was time they move into their respective universities:

Despite loving one another,

Some things weren't working out for them.

Maybe it was the distance

That bothered them,

Or maybe something else.

They did not know why

But they were afraid to let it out,

They didn't want to lose each other.

They were so used to each other,

That even the thought of distance from the other,

Made them cry.

But they had to move out!

Their careers were equally important:

And they wanted to focus on it.

Then came the time,

They bid their final goodbye,

It was hard for them to accept that tragic reality.

"It feels impossible to welcome this upsetting newness,
Especially when one feels a lot.
Nevertheless, every phase has its ebb and flow.
Life has its way of pulling apart
As much as it can bring together;
But the worst are the goodbyes that follow."
That autumn was a happy day for both,
They graduated high school with flying colours,
Their joy, forever captured in a picture
Those four years had been amazing for them.
They were together,
They actually understood what love meant.
All the cherished memories flashed in front of their eyes.
It was more than four years of friendship,
Which is why they had such great understanding towards the
other.
More than four years of dating that,
Made them realise so many things about each other,
Made them comfortable with one another.
They weren't ready to leave all of this behind,
To start afresh for themselves,
But they knew that they had to do it.
They still had hopes,
At the back of their minds,
That they would reunite;
Only time and fate knew how it would play out.
They were, however, clueless about this -

That unknown future was the stab to their hearts.
A few weeks later,
As they helped one another pack their bags -
When there were only few days before they left…
They did every little thing,
That made them happy,
That which brought that cute smile on their faces.
They spent nights together talking about
How they've grown with each other,
How they have enhanced each other's personalities.
In those moments, both tried to keep their goodbyes
At a standstill, not wanting any sorrow,
All they wanted was the last of this to be a beautiful memory.
Before they finally left
All those precious little things,
They promised to cherish those memories.
They made the most of their last days together;
He still remembered the cold winter,
The goodbye was sorrowful and piercing.
She was the one who was leaving first.
She was ready to kick-start her new life.
She wanted to achieve a lot in life.
And so did he:
But all he could think of
As he dropped her at the airport,
Was how much they would miss each other.
She looked as beautiful as the starry night sky.

He just couldn't take his eyes off her.
Neither could she,
He watched as she tried to keep her tears in.
The final call: and she boarded the flight.
A week later he too left,
He did miss her – a lot;
But he was ready to start afresh too.
Both, as soon as they got into university
Indulged in their studies;
Their focus, more on their careers.
Meeting new people,
Interacting with new people,
Was difficult for the two.
But they certainly figured
Slow and steadily:
How to get used to this new life, away from each other.
They still missed each other,
But texting each other and knowing they were doing well,
Gave them an inner satisfaction.
Life had pretty much got back to normal for the two.
And then came something
Which hit her hard.
Those three years, they focused on their studies,
They healed.
They bettered their lives.
One fine day,
She saw a picture of him with a girl,

That picture pretty much made it obvious:

That there was some kind of liking,

Towards him by the girl.

But she wasn't ready to accept what she saw.

All of those good times hit her back,

Tears went rolling down her eyes onto her cheeks.

She missed him a lot.

She feared to ask him about that girl,

Since they promised to stay friends,

Even after they broke up.

She thought she had no right to ask him

About his romantic life,

Because she wasn't his girlfriend anymore.

But she wanted to talk it out with someone,

She wanted to vent out things,

She didn't want to keep things inside her.

She finally mustered up the courage,

And asked him about that girl.

"Is something there between the two of you?"

He replied with an honest answer:

"She has feelings for me,

But I don't know whether I feel the same for her"

It had been really long,

Since they had gone through their breakup;

But they hadn't really gotten over each other.

Maybe their love was so strong,

Their relationship, so healthy that it matured -

To an unwavering one through the course of time.
But they were far apart from each other,
And while they wanted to get back,
Situations weren't in their favour.
They were scared.
They didn't want any miscommunications.
They didn't want to fight every other day.
Keeping these things in mind,
They tried to forget each other,
For their own good.
Their mental health was disturbed,
Every small thing around them,
Reminded them of their relationship;
Every ice cream shop reminded them of
How they would meet up for some quality time,
Just to check on how their lives were going on.
Those talks in that cozy corner,
Just to give each other emotional support.
Just to hug out their pain.
Walking by the streets,
Passing by the green trees,
Wishing upon shooting stars.
Just the two of them,
Hand in hand,
Forgetting all the negativity that came with life.
Those school days,
Where their friendship blossomed,

To an impeccable relationship.
They had come a long way,
And drifting apart,
Just did not seem right.
They had tried talking on calls,
But they couldn't connect
The way they used to, without the distance.
They had reached a place where silence was awkward
Something felt incomplete.
Things did not seem as it was in the past, back then.
They would try not to be upset with the other,
But they couldn't handle the missing that came with the distance.
He'd shed a tear or two, and she would break down inconsolably.
Finally, they had decided
That this had to stop –
It was a lot on them mentally and emotionally.
They couldn't take it anymore,
One call ended things completely.
They had decided that they would not even speak for a while,
A mutual decision: Neither wanted to take But had to take;
They weren't happy with what they had done,
The moment they disconnected the call,
More than their eyes crying out, their hearts did.
But they diverted their focus on their university: To achieve something big in life,

So that they were proud of themselves later on.

Chapter 03: To Love Again

Two years had passed since then;

Both had post-graduated with excellent grades,

In their respective field of studies.

In spite of the emotional breakdowns

Both had gone through,

They did not let it get in the way of their education.

Now had come the time they were working,

Almost forgetting their past,

Both only cherished the memories.

They began to meet new people.

Tried to open up to them.

Laughed things out with friends.

But somewhere deep down,

The talks were not that comforting,

As it was when they used to have it.

Their life seemed perfect again,

They eventually seemed to have found

Their people and learned to laugh again.

It had been over two years,

Since they had been working

And been in different relationships

Their respective partners,

Wanted to settle down soon

But the two did not seem to be ready.

Feeling it was too big of a step,

Something told them they were not ready,

They felt they needed time.

Both were at a point contemplating,

Whether this was the happiness,

That was deserving.

Then came the day,

The day fate had in mind,

For them to meet again.

Co-incidentally,

They bumped into the other,

At an office meeting.

They could not get their eyes off the other:

Couldn't believe they were standing in front of the other,

After all these years.

Memories flashed, and a hidden hope

Of coming back together

Burned deep within.

That deep love and profound respect,

They could sense it,

It flooded and overwhelmed.

After the meeting was over,

They both took a break at the office balcony

And shared a cup of coffee like old times.

They could feel the gentle breeze

This was their thing -

This was what made their moods jovial.

There was a slight awkward silence,

He took the step to break the ice,

Their lives had changed.

Both were successful in life,

Both were attractive,

No longer were they young teens.

Everything had changed since then,

Except for that one thing: the love

Even they were not aware of what hey still had for the other.

They went on to have a deep conversation,

They spoke their hearts out with that same comfort,

They mentioned their partners.

They pretended to not get affected by the fact

That they had different partners,

But jealousy ripped them inside.

That love could still be read in their eyes,

Even now as they faced each other

As accomplished people.

They decided to meet up for dinner,

And soon, those dinner nights became more frequent.

They knew that they still had feelings for the other.

Deep down, they wanted to give their relationship another chance.

Whilst both didn't want to hurt their partners,

But they had to look out for their own satisfaction.

They decided to end things with their respective partners,

By giving them valid reasons

Not wanting to hurt their feelings by not being loyal to them.

They were so excited to start this new journey again.
It did not seem that they had been away from each other
For five long years.
They were surprised,
By the fact, that this distance,
Had not changed anything between the two.
They still remembered
Those minute details about each other.
And there was immense happiness when they laughed together.
They felt that everything lost,
Was coming back together,
Everything was in its rightful place again.
The three years were mind-blowing;
Since the time they got back together,
They bloomed, and were content.
Together, they purchased their dream house.
They decorated every nook and corner of every room -
Just like they had dreamt, in their high school days.
They couldn't even start to believe,
That all those dreams together,
Were now coming to life.
This time, reality hit them differently;
There were tears rolling down her eyes:
But this time, these were tears of joy.
More than grateful, they now appreciated
Their reunion:

Everything was just as they wished back then.

The light drizzle of the rains pattered -

A few droplets on the window pane;

The scene was captivating: she looked poised, watching it.

Now was the perfect time, he thought,

His fists clenched in his pant pockets,

One of them holding a tiny blue velvet box.

She comfortably laid on his shoulders in her pyjamas,

He wanted this to be extra special for her,

He was anxious and a felt a tinge of fear.

His heart beat rapidly,

Felt like he had run miles

A bead of sweat trickled down his forehead.

Questions reeled at the back of his mind,

Nevertheless, he was more than prepared.

Swiftly sliding away and onto one knee,

Within an instant, he held that tiny box,

She was surprised, the emotions flickered on her face.

He stared into her brown wide eyes,

The moment he popped open the box

Light shone on her face,

Her reactions captivated him and gave him the confidence:

"I cannot imagine even a second of my life without you,

I want to spend the rest of my life with you,

Will you marry me?"

As he spoke these lines

She was emotional, tears and without any hesitation,

An immediate reply: a squealing yes!

He got up and hugged her tightly, not wanting to let her go,

Finally, after all the ups and downs they had faced in life,

They were standing in front of the other, as future husband and wife

Their engagement was announced to their families,

Soon they were engaged and decided upon a wedding date,

Their wedding ceremony was traditional - vows made for eternity.

It was a beautiful wedding alongside a beach,

He could no longer hold back his tears,

When he saw her walk down the aisle towards him in her white gown.

He was in awe of her charm,

He looked deeply into her,

Lifted her veil back, and held her hands.

He looked classy and handsome in his suit,

They exchanged rings; they exchanged vows,

They promised to be with each other, their entire life.

The kiss on their lips sealed those promises.

Picking her up in his arms,

He vowed again he would be by her side.

Two years later,

They were blessed with twins,

As a result of their love.

Looking at their daughter and son play,

They realized that they

Had come a long way;

They made it this far together,

Because of their love, towards the other.

A love which had truly grown and matured.

Nothing could break them apart -

Through thick and thin

They had each other's back.

They were now a family,

Feeling fortunate,

Knowing that nothing could tear them apart.

Chapter2

TO LOSE

It was time they move into their respective universities:

Despite loving one another,

Some things weren't working out for them.

Maybe it was the distance

That bothered them,

Or maybe something else.

They did not know why

But they were afraid to let it out,

They didn't want to lose each other.

They were so used to each other,

That even the thought of distance from the other,

Made them cry.

But they had to move out!

Their careers were equally important:

And they wanted to focus on it.

Then came the time,

They bid their final goodbye,

It was hard for them to accept that tragic reality.

"It feels impossible to welcome this upsetting newness,

Especially when one feels a lot.

Nevertheless, every phase has its ebb and flow.

Life has its way of pulling apart

As much as it can bring together;

But the worst are the goodbyes that follow."

That autumn was a happy day for both,

They graduated high school with flying colours,

Their joy, forever captured in a picture

Those four years had been amazing for them.

They were together,

They actually understood what love meant.

All the cherished memories flashed in front of their eyes.

It was more than four years of friendship,

Which is why they had such great understanding towards the other.

More than four years of dating that,

Made them realise so many things about each other,

Made them comfortable with one another.

They weren't ready to leave all of this behind,

To start afresh for themselves,

But they knew that they had to do it.

They still had hopes,

At the back of their minds,

That they would reunite;

Only time and fate knew how it would play out.

They were, however, clueless about this -

That unknown future was the stab to their hearts.

A few weeks later,

As they helped one another pack their bags -
When there were only few days before they left…
They did every little thing,
That made them happy,
That which brought that cute smile on their faces.
They spent nights together talking about
How they've grown with each other,
How they have enhanced each other's personalities.
In those moments, both tried to keep their goodbyes
At a standstill, not wanting any sorrow,
All they wanted was the last of this to be a beautiful memory.
Before they finally left
All those precious little things,
They promised to cherish those memories.
They made the most of their last days together;
He still remembered the cold winter,
The goodbye was sorrowful and piercing.
She was the one who was leaving first.
She was ready to kick-start her new life.
She wanted to achieve a lot in life.
And so did he:
But all he could think of
As he dropped her at the airport,
Was how much they would miss each other.
She looked as beautiful as the starry night sky.
He just couldn't take his eyes off her.
Neither could she,

He watched as she tried to keep her tears in.
The final call: and she boarded the flight.
A week later he too left,
He did miss her – a lot;
But he was ready to start afresh too.
Both, as soon as they got into university
Indulged in their studies;
Their focus, more on their careers.
Meeting new people,
Interacting with new people,
Was difficult for the two.
But they certainly figured
Slow and steadily:
How to get used to this new life away from each other.
They still missed each other,
But texting each other and knowing they were doing well,
Gave them an inner satisfaction.
Life had pretty much got back to normal for the two.
And then came something
Which hit her hard.
Those three years, they focused on their studies,
They healed.
They bettered their lives.
One fine day,
She saw a picture of him with a girl,
That picture pretty much made it obvious:
That there was some kind of liking,

Towards him by the girl.
But she wasn't ready to accept what she saw.
All of those good times hit her back,
Tears went rolling down her eyes onto her cheeks.
She missed him a lot.
She feared to ask him about that girl,
Since they promised to stay friends,
Even after they broke up.
She thought she had no right to ask him
About his romantic life,
Because she wasn't his girlfriend anymore.
But she wanted to talk it out with someone,
She wanted to vent out things,
She didn't want to keep things inside her.
She finally mustered up the courage,
And asked him about that girl.
"Is something there between the two of you?"
He replied with an honest answer:
"She has feelings for me,
But I don't know whether I feel the same for her"
It had been really long,
Since they had gone through their breakup;
But they hadn't really gotten over each other.
Maybe their love was so strong,
Their relationship, so healthy that it matured -
To an unwavering one through the course of time.
But they were far apart from each other,

And while they wanted to get back,

Situations weren't in their favour.

They were scared.

They didn't want any miscommunications.

They didn't want to fight every other day.

Keeping these things in mind,

They tried to forget each other,

For their own good.

Their mental health was disturbed,

Every small thing around them,

Reminded them of their relationship;

Every ice cream shop reminded them of

How they would meet up for some quality time,

Just to check on how their lives were going on.

Those talks in that cozy corner,

Just to give each other emotional support.

Just to hug out their pain.

Walking by the streets,

Passing by the green trees,

Wishing upon shooting stars.

Just the two of them,

Hand in hand,

Forgetting all the negativity that came with life.

Those school days,

Where their friendship blossomed,

To an impeccable relationship.

They had come a long way,

And drifting apart,
Just did not seem right.
They had tried talking on calls,
But they couldn't connect
The way they used to, without the distance.
They had reached a place where silence was awkward
Something felt incomplete.
Things did not seem as it was in the past, back then.
They would try not to be upset with the other,
But they couldn't handle the missing that came with the distance.
He'd shed a tear or two, and she would break down inconsolably.
Finally, they had decided
That this had to stop –
It was a lot on them mentally and emotionally.
They couldn't take it anymore,
One call ended things completely.
They had decided that they would not even speak for a while,
A mutual decision: Neither wanted to take But had to take;
They weren't happy with what they had done,
The moment they disconnected the call,
More than their eyes crying out, their hearts did.
But they diverted their focus on their university: To achieve something big in life,
So that they were proud of themselves later on.

Chapter3

TO LOVE AGAIN

Two years had passed since then;
Both had post-graduated with excellent grades,
In their respective field of studies.
In spite of the emotional breakdowns
Both had gone through,
They did not let it get in the way of their education.
Now had come the time they were working,
Almost forgetting their past,
Both only cherished the memories.
They began to meet new people.
Tried to open up to them.
Laughed things out with friends.
But somewhere deep down,
The talks were not that comforting,
As it was when they used to have it.
Their life seemed perfect again,
They eventually seemed to have found
Their people and learned to laugh again.
It had been over two years,
Since they had been working

And been in different relationships

Their respective partners,

Wanted to settle down soon

But the two did not seem to be ready.

Feeling it was too big a step,

Something told them they were not ready,

They felt they needed time.

Both were at a point contemplating,

Whether this was the happiness,

That was deserving.

Then came the day,

The day fate had in mind,

For them to meet again.

Co-incidentally,

They bumped into the other,

At an office meeting.

They could not get their eyes off the other:

Couldn't believe they were standing in front of the other,

After all these years.

Memories flashed, and a hidden hope

Of coming back together

Burned deep within.

That deep love and profound respect,

They could sense it,

It flooded and overwhelmed.

After the meeting was over,

They both took a break at the office balcony

And shared a cup of coffee like old times.
They could feel the gentle breeze
This was their thing -
This was what made their moods jovial.
There was a slight awkward silence,
He took the step to break the ice,
Their lives had changed.
Both were successful in life,
Both were attractive,
No longer were they young teens.
Everything had changed since then,
Except for that one thing: the love
Even they were not aware of they still had for the other.
They went on to have a deep conversation,
They spoke their hearts out with that same comfort,
They mentioned their partners.
They pretended to not get affected by the fact
That they had different partners,
But jealousy ripped them inside.
That love could still be read in their eyes,
Even now as they faced each other
As accomplished people.
They decided to meet up for dinner,
And soon, those dinner nights became more frequent.
They knew that they still had feeling for the other.
Deep down, they wanted to give their relationship another chance.

Whilst both didn't want to hurt their partners,
They had to look out for their own satisfaction.
They decided to end things with their respective partners,
By giving them valid reasons
Not wanting to hurt their feelings by not being loyal to them.
They were so excited to start this new journey again.
It did not seem that they had been away from each other
For five long years.
They were surprised,
By the fact, that this distance,
Had not changed anything between the two.
They still remembered
Those minute details about each other.
And there was immense happiness when they laughed together.
They felt that everything lost,
Was coming back together,
Everything was in its rightful place again.
The three years were mind-blowing; mSince the time they got back together,
They bloomed, and were content.
Together, they purchased their dream house.
They decorated every nook and corner of every room -
Just like they had dreamt, in their high school days.
They couldn't even start to believe,
That all those dreams together,
Were now coming to life.

This time reality hit them differently;

There were tears rolling down her eyes:

But this time these were tears of joy.

More than grateful, they now appreciated

Their reunion:

Everything was just as they wished back then.

The light drizzle of the rains pattered -

A few droplets on the window pane;

The scene was captivating: she looked poised, watching it.

Now was the perfect time, he thought,

His fists clenched in his pant pockets,

One of them holding a tiny blue velvet box.

She comfortably laid on his shoulders in her pyjamas,

He wanted this to be extra special for her,

He was anxious and a felt a tinge of fear.

His heart beat rapidly,

Felt like he had run miles

A bead of sweat trickled down his forehead.

Questions reeled at the back of his mind, Nevertheless, he was

more than prepared.

Swiftly sliding away and onto one knee,

Within an instant, he held that tiny box,

She was surprised, the emotions flickered on her face.

He stared into her brown wide eyes,

The moment he popped open the box

Light shone on her face,

Her reactions captivated him and gave him the confidence:

"I cannot imagine even a second of my life without you,

I want to spend the rest of my life with you,

Will you marry me?"

As he spoke these lines

She was emotional, tears and

An immediate reply: a squealing yes!

He got up and hugged her tightly, not wanting to let her go,

Finally, after all the ups and downs they had faced in life,

They were standing in front of the other, as future husband and wife

Their engagement was announced to their families,

Soon they were engaged and decided upon a wedding date,

Their wedding ceremony was traditional - vows made for eternity.

It was a beautiful wedding alongside a beach,

He could no longer hold back his tears,

When he saw her walk towards him in her white gown.

He was in awe of her charm,

He looked deeply into her,

Lifted her veil back, and held her hands.

He looked classy and handsome in his suit,

They exchanged rings; they exchanged vows,

They promised to be with each other, their entire life.

The kiss on their lips sealed those promises.

Picking her up in his arms,

He vowed again he would be by her side.

Two years later,

They were blessed with twins,

As a result of their love.

Looking at their daughter and son play,

They realized that they

Had come a long way;

They made it this far together,

Because of their love, towards the other.

A love which had truly grown and matured.

Nothing could break them apart -

Through thick and thin

They had each other's back.

They were now a family,

Feeling fortunate,

Knowing that nothing could tear them apart.

EPILOGUE:

Love: a simple four-letter word.

It can create a lot of complications:

When not understood properly.

Only a person genuinely in love

Can for certain understand,

Its true definition.

It's a feeling, a desire,

One that has a need to be reciprocated,

And is also felt deep within.

It's the most exceptional thing

That will happen to you,

In a world of pain and stress.

Once you truly experience it,

Make sure you learn to appreciate it,

And not make it suffocating.

Love: She is one of the best feelings.

Love: She changes you for good.

Love: She is powerful.

Love: She teaches you to be kind.

Love: She is an everlasting emotion.